McGrath MATH

TEDDY BEAR
COUNTING

Barbara Barbieri McGrath
Illustrated by Tim Nihoff

Charlesbridge

To Judy O'Malley, for bearing with me—B. B. M.

To my big sister, Debi, the one
you can always count on—T. N.

Text copyright © 2010 by Barbara Barbieri McGrath
Illustrations copyright © 2010 by Tim Nihoff
All rights reserved, including the right of reproduction
in whole or in part in any form. Charlesbridge
and colophon are registered trademarks of
Charlesbridge Publishing, Inc.

Published by Charlesbridge
85 Main Street
Watertown, MA 02472
(617) 926-0329
www.charlesbridge.com

Printed in China
(hc) 10 9 8 7 6 5 4 3 2 1
(sc) 10 9 8 7 6 5 4 3 2 1

Library of Congress Cataloging-in-Publication Data
McGrath, Barbara Barbieri, 1954–
    Teddy bear counting / Barbara Barbieri McGrath ;
illustrated by Tim Nihoff.
        p. cm.
    Summary: Teddy bears introduce numbers from one to
twelve, as well as colors and shapes.
    ISBN 978-1-58089-215-5 (reinforced for library use)
    ISBN 978-1-58089-216-2 (softcover)
[1. Stories in rhyme. 2. Teddy bears—Fiction. 3. Counting.
4. Shape. 5. Color.] I. Nihoff, Tim, ill.
II. Title.
PZ8.3.M459584Te 2010
[E]—dc22   2008025339

Illustrations hand drawn digitally in Adobe Photoshop
Display type set in Animated Gothic and
    text type set in Century Schoolbook
Color separations by Chroma Graphics, Singapore
Manufactured by Regent Publishing Services, Hong Kong
Printed September 2009 in ShenZhen, Guangdong, China
Production supervision by Brian G. Walker
Designed by Susan Mallory Sherman

Bears tumble in.

Get ready, get set.

This counting book is
the most playful yet!

Bears say their colors.

It's easy to do.

"I'm red!"   "And I'm yellow!"

"I'm green!"

"Well, I'm blue!"

1

First is one red.

Yellow makes two.

A green bear is three.

Count four with this blue.

4

One red marches in

5

to make five bears in all.

When yellow joins, too,

six teddies sit tall.

6

A green one arrives.
Seven now form a group.

7

Then a blue comes along,

making eight in the troop.

8

One bear cartwheels in

to make nine in the line.

9

Another drops by,

and ten teddies look fine.

10

Ten teddies line up,

then bend low to bow.

11

To count to eleven
add one teddy now.

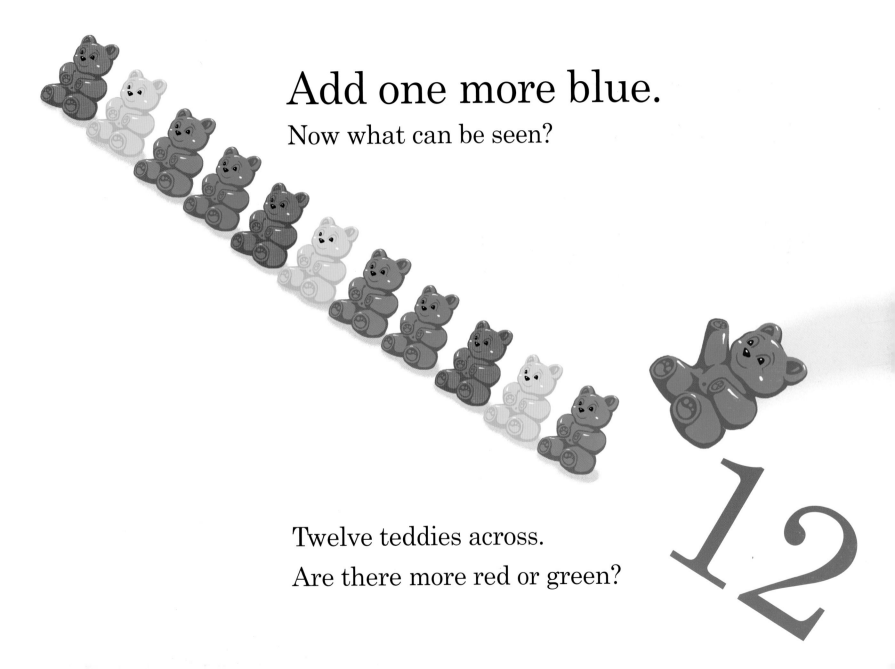

Add one more blue.

Now what can be seen?

Twelve teddies across.

Are there more red or green?

12

A set of twelve teddies

makes a rainbow for you.

Six bears can choose partners—

2+2+2+2+2+2=12

that's six sets of two.

The bears move around

and make three sets of four.

Count up how many:

just twelve and no more.

$4+4+4=12$

Teddies all dancing

make four sets of three,
and still only twelve
are all we can see.

3+3+3+3=12

Two sets of six say,

"How do you do?"

6+6=12

Since that went so well,
they try something new.

Bears hop,

skip, and jump,

and fly through the air.
When they all land
they make a big square.

The bears shape a circle

that goes round and round.

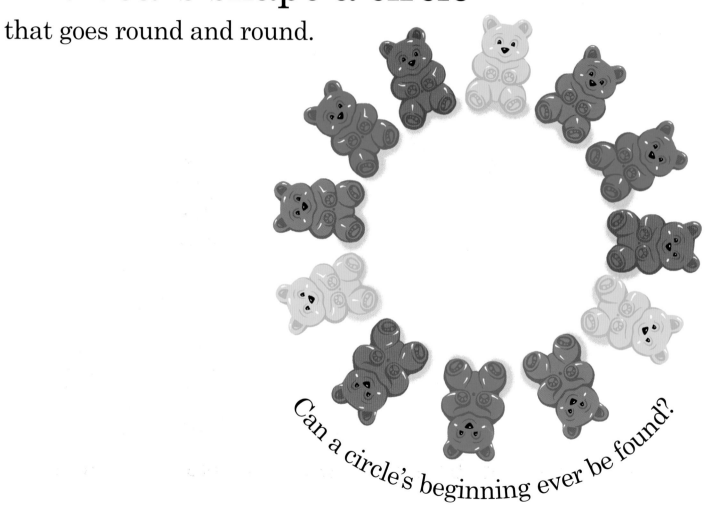

Can a circle's beginning ever be found?

A triangle's next

before these bears stop.

They give it three sides, with one bear on the top!

One bear of each color

won't risk being late.

Four bears have to go.

That leaves only eight.

$$12-4=8$$

More teddies are leaving.

It's bear moving day.

With places to go,

two more walk away.

$8-2=6$

Six bears remain

with little to do.

Say so long to four. . . .

We're left with just two.

 $6-4=2$

One little teddy

runs away fast.

Say hello to the bear
who chose to be last.

$2-1=1$

The bear stands alone.

What a brave little hero.

When he trots away,

there are none. That means zero!

0

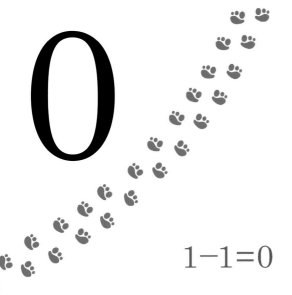

$1-1=0$

Bye, counting bears.

They're gone now, but when

the teddies come back,   they'll   all   play   again!

The bears had great fun. They tried something new.
To help them remember, let's have a review!

COLORS

red

yellow

green

blue

SHAPES

□
square

○
circle

△
triangle

NUMBERS

1	one	5	five	9	nine
2	two	6	six	10	ten
3	three	7	seven	11	eleven
4	four	8	eight	12	twelve

SETS OF TWELVE

1 set

2 sets

3 sets

4 sets

6 sets